The Day Ann Finds Out Dad's Big Secret

R.A. Berry

AuthorHouse™
1663 Liberty Drive
Bloomington, IN 47403
www.authorhouse.com
Phone: 833-262-8899

Because of the dynamic nature of the Internet, any web addresses or links contained in this book may have changed
since publication and may no longer be valid. The views expressed in this work are solely those of the author and do
not necessarily reflect the views of the publisher, and the publisher hereby disclaims any responsibility for them.

Any people depicted in stock imagery provided by Getty Images are models,
and such images are being used for illustrative purposes only.
Certain stock imagery © Getty Images.

This book is printed on acid-free paper.

ISBN: 978-1-4343-8191-0 (sc)

Print information available on the last page.

Published by AuthorHouse 09/29/2022

authorHOUSE®

Dedicated to Tab and A.J.

Ann was tired from a long day at school. She just wanted to take a nap. Afterwards she would do her homework and have supper. When supper was finished, they would watch one television show and then go to bed. This wasn't so exciting to Ann.

Ann's daddy liked ice cream. Her daddy walked into the room and said, "Ann would you like to go with me to the store to get some ice cream?" Ann jumped up and down. She loved getting out of the house especially with her dad. She yells, "Alright!" Sharon, Ann's big sister asks if she can go too. Dad says, "I reckon, that's southern for yes, Sharon you can come too."

The girls rush to get their sweaters. After getting into the truck, they began to stretch their necks trying to see over the dashboard. They can hardly hold in their excitement. They didn't get to ride in dad's work truck often. As they traveled, the lights from the other cars stared at them as they passed by. Dad drives fast so they can get back in time for their favorite show. It is pitch black outside as they travel down the long lonely road. Their house is a long way from the main road. The lights from the dashboard help the girls see inside the truck. They give each other a silent smile and giggle.

While riding along, dad reminded them again to stay in school and do the best they can in class. He always promised to see them through at least until they get out of high school. "I'm going to work hard to get you all out of school then you're on your own," he declares. Sometimes Ann would feel very sad as he would talk to them because he would tell them how he wasn't allowed to attend school so that he could work on the farm with his father. "I had to walk many miles to school even in the snow when I was young," dad would say. After a while, my father made me stop going to school because I had to work on the farm with him and I don't want you to come up like I did, you hear me?" By the time he had just gotten started with his story, Ann could see the lights from the supermarket.

Ann and Sharon took a deep breath. They could hardly wait to go inside with their dad. Dad surprised them and told them to go inside together. "Alone!" said Ann. "Alone", replied dad. The girls looked at each other and smiled. "You'd better hurry up. The store is about to close," said Dad. The girls opened the door and climbed out of the truck.

"Oh! What kind of ice cream do you want?" Ann said with a big smile on her face. "Red Cap ice cream," he replied smiling back at her. The girls repeated the name as they walked so they wouldn't forget it.

Once inside the store, Ann and Sharon headed straight for the freezer section where the ice cream is kept. The store was cold and quiet. There weren't many people inside the store. Their teeth chattered as they peered over the counter looking for the Red Cap ice cream. They looked carefully but didn't see it. Neither girl wanted to disappoint their father.

They argued, "You go tell him!" Ann said. "No, You go tell him." Sharon snapped back. "Nope, I'm not going, you go. I'm too little to go outside by myself!" Ann said with a smirk on her face. They agreed to try again. Sharon pointing her finger suggested, "Let's split up. You go on the other end of the counter and I'll go on this end. We'll meet in the middle. This way we won't miss anything". Ann hurried to the other end. They searched and searched as hard as they could but no Red Cap ice cream.

Now they had to go tell dad that they couldn't find his favorite ice cream. "Go tell dad that we can't find it", said Ann. Sharon quickly replied, "Not on your life!" "Well, I'm not going and nobody wanted you to come anyway!" Ann said quietly wiping away tears.

Mr. Brown the store manager listened as the girls tried to decide who should break the news to their dad. Mr. Brown began looking. The girls like this because he was tall and could see better from up there. Just as he began to look the girls heard the announcer say, "Please finish you shopping, the store will be closing in 5 minutes." Mr. Brown decided he would go outside and tell dad. They were good friends. The girls were so happy.

Mr. Brown went to the truck. "Mr. James, the girls can't find the ice cream you want. Can you please come inside and find it because the store will be closing soon".

Mr. James came inside the store and goes directly to the freezer section. He walks over to the girls and shows them a box of ice cream with the "red cap" on the front.
To everyone's surprise, the ice cream wasn't called red cap ice cream but instead "Really Good" ice cream. Ann looked at Sharon. Sharon looked at Ann. Neither girl said a word. The store manager didn't seem surprised.

Each of them pondered in their minds for a while what had happened. When they got into the truck, they didn't say a word all the way home. After getting into bed, Ann finally whispered, "Sharon, did you know daddy can't read?" Sharon replied very softly, "I do now." By this time both girls had tears running down the side of their little faces. They immediately turned and gave each other a big hug as they dozed off to sleep.

The next day, Ann couldn't think about anything else. She had to find a way to help her dad. Then she thought to herself, I can read to him and show him words. Maybe this way he can remember them. She thought this would be a good idea. That night, Ann bought dad's favorite book over to him. His favorite book was the bible. She began to read from a chapter in a book called Psalms. Dad liked that a lot. For the next few months, Ann would read to him every night.

After a while, Dad began to remember many of the words and could read by himself. He would take Ann on many trips with him to read for him and help him. They would read signs, menus, and instructions. Ann became a much better reader by helping her dad. Dad was very happy. Ann was happy also.

The End

About the Author

Roz Berry is the mother of two wonderful children, Tabitha and A.J. She began her educational career after becoming a PTA president. She always wanted to help others in some way. She received her B.A. in Psychology from the College of New Rochelle. She has a Master's Degree from Queens College in Elementary and Early Childhood Education. She has a School District Administration and School Administrator's Supervisor's Certificate in Advanced Studies from the state of New York. She is a facilitator for the New Teacher's Orientation of New York. She has been featured on NBC nightly news. She is a member of Phi Delta Kappa, Who's Who of America's Teacher (2005), Who's Who of America's Executive and Professional Women and received many honors for her work in education. She was given a teaching job at an elementary school in Queens where she has become more of a "mom" to the little ones as well as a teacher/school based mentor.

Printed in the United States
by Baker & Taylor Publisher Services